Maybe He Doesn't Hit You

poetry

by

Beth Mattson

Dedicated to your mom, as always.

This Is My Nest

This is where we snuggle
Where I pick mice
Limb from limb
This is where we sleep
And wake

<u>Flying</u>
You have to
Work at it
Like swimming.
You can't
Just float.
You'll sink.

Accidental Boob Selfie

I was taking artsy pics
Of wild violets in the yard
Tasteful
Nicely composed
Nobody wants to see either

<u>Easter Morning</u>
Church breakfast
And lacy frills
At least my boy in pearls
My girl in a bowtie
Discount chocolate tomorrow

Early Spring Clay
Radishes are ecstatic
Peas & beans are fine
Potatoes will pull their shit together
Carrots just told me to go fuck myself

<u>Land Amniotes</u>
No more water
For fertilization.
Chica chica
Bow wow.

Child Mortality
Even in the fossil record
The phrase
Infant skull
Strikes fear
Into my
Bony heart.

Mother Love

The sharpest teeth
And rawest nails
And sorest throat
And the sharpest teeth
The sharpest teeth
The sharpest teeth
The sharpest teeth
On behalf of chubby legs
And sticky hands

Ursula K Le Guin
And in this rich, seemly, orderly,
Strange Court,
I felt myself to be a goatherd
Born and bred.

Mosaic
Can it be
My job
To smash
And break
All the glass
And pottery

Bloody Apes
How do we
Survive as a species
When all we ever do
Is harry harlow each other
Over and over again
Would you like the terry cloth
Or bare wire?

Things To Hide Behind
Rage
Refrigerator
Anger
Table
Door
Corner
Resentment
Ire
Box
Curtain
Thick Skull

Unsuspecting
The dashing barista
Whom he flirts with
While wasting money
On croissants not diapers
Tells me he's a great guy.

Abuse Post Script

After he slept in
He yelled at me
For using the oven wrong.

We Don't Listen To Women

Nope nope nope nope nope nope nope nope nope nope nope nope
nope nope nope nope nope nope nope nope nope nope nope nope

Nope nope nope nope nope nope nope nope
nope nope nope nope nope nope nope nope nope nope nope nope
nope nope nope nope nope nope nope nope nope nope nope nope
nope nope nope nope nope nope nope nope nope nope nope nope
nope nope nope nope nope nope nope nope nope

Nope nope nope nope nope nope nope nope nope nope nope
nope nope nope nope nope nope nope nope nope nope nope nope
nope nope nope nope nope   Nope nope nope nope

Nope nope nope nope nope nope nope nope nope nope nope nope
nope nope nope nope nope nope

NOOOOOOOOOOOOOOOOOOOOOOOOOOOPE

Unreliable Narrator
I hope your gross toe is better
I've moved on
This isn't a love letter
Not lust either

<u>That Little Hand Twist</u>
Yes, keep reading
A lot of these
Are literary devices
Used poorly

<u>My Lumberjack Viking</u>
I don't want to move on
Back to real life
With less lumber
And fewer ships

Don't Call Me
If I am like trying
To drink from a firehose
Lose my number
Be thirsty

The Virgin And The Whore

Well just one
Of those
I guess
But does that mean
I can't hold your hand
And eat peanut butter
And jelly?

<u>Personal Velocity</u>
I'm ready now.
Why doesn't it all happen
Immediately?

Gemini

Always looking for my twin
Today, can it be you?

The Ocean
What a beautiful,
Beautiful,
BeauuUUuuuuUUUuutiful
Deathtrap.

<u>Life Story</u>
As told on a hot day
I am smelly
From my adventures.

Discovering Sex With Women

I literally failed chemistry,
But figuratively
I got an A+

<u>Peak Zucchini Season</u>
My family was not concerned
By my happy dance
But by the attempt
At singing that followed

First Pool Day
Just wading in the yard
Turkeys wooing in woods
Moths waking up
Clouds gathering
More 40 and 50 to come
But pool inflated
Sunscreen on

Because I Have Children
Why are there
Chips in the bed?
Ponies in the bath?
Teeth in my lips?

More Than Once A Day

She asks if I can pick her up
I can't I love you I miss you
I am sorry
You'll be ok
And then she hangs up

<u>Eleanor</u>
Is soft and spicy
Full of adventure
Where were you, child?
Talking to owls.
Oh, Of course

<u>Lalore</u>
She finally pronounced
His real name
While he was at school
"I love my brother,
Charlie."

It Doesn't Count

Until he knocks you out
In a hotel elevator camera
And then they'll still blame you
For staying.

<u>Your Love Narrative</u>
Of a noble jerk
Doing the right thing
In the end
Makes my complete failure
So much worse.

Boudica
Does not tell you
Of her true sorrow
Or rage
Else you would weep
And claw

<u>May You Never Know</u>
What this is really like
It's so much worse
Than you can imagine

Maybe He Doesn't Hit You

But he makes out with
Not one
But many others
On your wedding day
After everything else
You only find out years later

Maybe he doesn't hit you
But he blames his depression
His headaches
His suicide
His firings
His cheating
His everything
All on you

Maybe he doesn't hit you
But he forbids the thermostat
Changing the windows' cracks
And spoons for lunch
He'll get drunk
And lock you out
Away from crying baby

Maybe he doesn't hit you
But he says things
Like "fiscal dynamite -- BOOM!"
With glee in his eyes
And rage in his voice
About babies' daycare

Maybe he doesn't hit you
But he has an ego
the size of your wounds
And listens to no one
Unless they're a
Sparkling trophy,
Naked, rich and gold

Maybe he doesn't hit you
But he has major mental health
And morality issues
That are dangerous, careless,
Calloused, concealed
Soaked in expensive wine
And a really nice suit

Maybe he doesn't hit you
But he accuses you
Of gaslighting
Telling you of your PD
Ignoring the thoughtful feedback
From dozens over decades

Maybe he doesn't hit you
But he slams your hand
In the car door
In front of the kids
Tells them all it was an accident
Like all the other assaults
He doesn't remember

Maybe he doesn't hit you
But he reads this and scoffs
Laughs at you and the things
That you started off whispering

<u>Survivor So Far</u>
Victims
Are all dead.
I'm not.

Weening

When I was small
I forgot my favorite blankly
On a long road trip
This is harder.

<u>Abstinate</u>
Condoms are too thin.
I want titanium between us.

<u>The Real J Jones</u>
Kilgrave won't stop
And I can't break his neck

<u>We Told You</u>
After each fresh tragedy
A woman
Or chorus of women
Standing with fists clenched
Teeth also
Hoarse
from yelling
I told you
I TOLD you
I TOLD YOU
All about him

Michael, Trayvon, Sandra, Etc.
The next time that you
Incorrectly fear for your own self
Please don't shoot a black kid.

<u>Aleppo</u>
My heart has been
With you
And broken
For years now

Terrifying Book
Another author had a
Horrible dream
And bothered to write it all down
Lucky you
Readers never sleep

The Things They Carried
I forget
How pages can help
Or smithereen
Shred
Blow apart
Rip and tear
Bleed from every word

Writers Will Eat You

We bite with our eyes
We chew with fingers and keys
We digest the lines
We shit entire lives

Tiny Beetle On Car Window
Every time I sing
Giggle or look at him
He raises his wings
Tough strong surviving
Sweet drive companion

Summer Volume

Lawn work, construction and
Kids screaming in hordes
Are so much louder
Than cold rain on the porch.

On The Belly
Fresh to Outside
Juicy
Slippery
Slimy
Bloody
Poopy
Milky
Warm
You won't ever
Be anyplace
As cozy
Ever again.

Momfinity
There is a story
About a child
Always being my baby.
It's all true.

<u>Cuddles</u>   .
Am I so comforting
That you would just
Close your eyes
And fall asleep
Holding my hand?
Yes.

<u>Susurrus</u>
Not the tongue
Cotton ears
Heavy blankets
Mixed with snow
Unwrap them
Fever breakers
You're not cold

Time I'd Never Get Back
Dieting
Shaving
Mopping
Mowing
Ironing
Church
Kissing ass
All quietly
No thanks

Quaaludes
If they're still a thing
Mommy wants in.

A Man Or A Book

The book
I say quickly
A woman or a book
Better, but still only friends
The family, warm fires
And those books
Always the books

Dove Deodorant Scent
Like Proustian cookies
Conjures visions
Of hot showers
And some women's armpits
That I licked
One Madeline

S'mores
A very simple recipe
So easy to burn the marshmallows
To a scorched, bloody crisp
I'm talking about heartache

<u>Girl Lube</u>
Is blood plasma.
Blood plasma is delicious.

<u>Egg Love</u>
Crack open
Let me swim in your yolk
Here's mine.

<u>Poetry Crush</u>
OMG
Your lips
On those words.

<u>Nerdy Sex</u>
I think
Cold feet
Are distracting so
I'm going
To keep my
Socks on.
You can too.

No Wishes
Nothing to see here
Not hopes
That you will nuzzle me
While I chop carrots
Spin and kiss
No sharp knife injuries either

Latest Disappointment
Why do camels
Carry so much straw?
Are they freaking freighters?
Why not bars of lead?
Or water?

<u>Unexpected Bad News</u>
I discussed it
With a bottle of wine
And bag of chocolate
We agree
It sucks

<u>Fifth Try</u>
Is not the charm,
Nope, it's not.
Maybe the sixth.

<u>Failure No. 100</u>
Fine.
I guess I'll go
Be good at something else.

Divorce Victory
It didn't feel good
Not for anybody

<u>Courtroom Tissues</u>
Strategically placed
For defendants
And prosecutors
Alike

A Narrative Of Healing
Was presented to me
On a platter
Why couldn't I reach it?

A Spell For Catharsis
May their dicks
Desiccate, mold
And fall off
May they believe
Weasel shit a cure
And eat all they can find

<u>Waiting for Reciprocity</u>
This is for you.
This is for you.
This is for you.
This is for you.
This is for you.
This is for you.

Today's Rhythm
Went to bed at 6
Brushed my teeth at 9
Did laundry at 11
Farted in the middle
Of the kitchen.
What do you care?

<u>Traditions</u>
I didn't know
But my father did
That's how close I am

Supper At Six
Dinner is at noon
On Sunday
After church
With pickles
And ham

Morning Drinking With My Parents
Love it
Cheers
They asked for bloody Marys
And now I have pledged
Earnestly
To someday tell their stories

Our Mailbox
Seed catalogs
Books and games
Science, the journal
Bills, of course
Sometimes a trampoline

Conflicting Scents
I sprinkled coyote piss
In the garden
And on my hands
Before I lit a candle
Wet dog back porch
Roast in oven

Apples Froze On The Tree
I collected them
And hit line drives
Into the weeds
Until my bat was sticky
And the low branches empty.

Duplex
I'll take one half
You the other
See you one
Out of every two
Hours
Minutes
Seconds
Shared laundry

Three Weeks Error
Those vitamins
Aren't sugar-free.
Those markers
Aren't dry erase.
That's not your name.
I don't love you
Anymore.

Life's About Timing

And two-way love
Which we don't have
So bye bye now
I won't see you around
Prolly
Glancing for confirmation
Yeah sigh

Claim Ticket
If you find yourself
In a coat check
Vallet line
Lost and found
Laundr'o'mat
Return yourself to me

Zodiac
How did the stars know
That I would be
A silly, verbal
Academic slut?

Slag
Is the same thing as Slut
Or molten splatters
So I guess I'm a fan.

<u>Trapeze</u>
I know there's a net
But I'm still in free fall

Ballast
I spend most of my time
Deeply grateful.
The other fifth is cold.

Don't Take My Catheter
No
I'm not ready
To hobble to the toilet yet
Everything still hurts

Birth

Such an average trauma.

Memory Span
One evening of joint custody
Kids out of my care
And I'd go back
To snuggle my babies.

Mom Morning
I nurse
I cook and clean and care
Before dawn
At 9am he says
Come on guys
Don't snuggle me
It's hard to get good sleep

Sad Piano Pandora
With a Christmas tree
But no babies
I cry myself to sleep
Or sing of eons of woes
Worse than mine

<u>I am Mama</u>
I shared blood
With my babies
He didn't share
Not nearly that much.

Yes I Can

So capable
So strong
I can handle it
I say
As he socially isolates me
Hurray for my muscles

<u>Fool Me</u>
Sixty
Million
Times
Shame on me.

<u>American Judicial</u>
White penis wins.
The end.

<u>My Depression Symptoms</u>
Familiar rage
Boring isolation
Back fat

PTSGeography
I need to know
Where you are
At all times
Wear a bell
It's too late
I can't hear it
Over the blasting foghorns

<u>Gory Accdiental Death</u>
I wouldn't wish that
On my worst enemy
But I do wish that
On my ex.

Long Sorrow

Nobody wants to listen
To me for as long
As my friends,
Beer and chocolate.
Grow more chins,
They wisely advise.

Confirmation Bias
You'll find
What you
Look for
This isn't
Double blind

Dreaming Of Shannon
When I'm asleep
We still sip coffee and wine
Hug, giggle
Play games
Talk about books
Try on costumes
Say goodbye

Locked Up Safe
It's not just that there
Would be consequences
There's no such thing
At all.

<u>Mommy</u>
She whispers
My warm name
The only reward

Undead Character
If the zombies ate my baby,
I'd let them eat me too.

Raw Hamburger
Marginalized hearts
Don't pick
No more salt, please
Not the hot grill

Young White Dudes
I gave them Lit
They still peed
Could have been blood
Could have been sperm
Could have been me
How will they ever learn?

Neither Our Educations
Nor silences
Will protect us
From traffic stops
Husbands,
Illnesses,
Hate,
Or nightclub bullets.

How Many Times
Have I heard "faggot!"
Been stared at in the bathroom
Flipped off by driving men
With gun racks and glares
Shots fired in Orlando?

Sad And Afraid
If you're not
If your mouth and arms
Aren't open to protest and protect
You are the problem
Of hate winning

I Am Not Yours
Not your saint
Not your demon
Not your hero
Not your villain
Not your wind
Not your water
I am all these things
But not for you
Just mine
All mine

It's Cold Here
Either my poop
Or my vagina just steamed
I can't tell which
Here, on an indoor potty

<u>Somebody Crumpling</u>
If you can't handle
This image, you
Shouldn't own a gun.
If you like this image,
You shouldn't own a gun.

We're The Worst

Forget humans.
I'm going to live with the bonobos.

Trauma Informed
I'm not being dramatic
Wouldn't you be scared
And angry too
If you were shut in a box
All taped up
With knives

<u>Heart Pounding</u>
Pretend to be careful
While running fast

Making Happy

A madhouse
Lined with silver
And lead

Monkey Bar Hands
There
I've proved that
I can still swing
Like a young ape
The blisters smell so good.
Iron and youth wreak.

Muscle Memory
Information not stored
In your brain.
Cerebellum?
Cortex?
Nope.
Not the command center.
We're all just fish.

Driving Spasm
Car seat feels so good
On my lower back
Has a built-in heating pad
Where else can we commute today?

No Cryogenics

If some eccentric rich people
Can freeze themselves,
Why can't some other nerds
Figure out how to fossilize me?

<u>Autoshop Coffee</u>
Was terrible yesterday
Worse today
Dregs from my cold cup holder
I needed it
I want more

Spider Gears
Not planetary.
Similar.
Limited slip.
Crawling all over each other.

Aunty Medicine
I can't read the translation
Smells like menthol
Sure I'll try it
Boom amazing
Involuntary nap
Wow
What was that?
I'm Cured

Blueberry Sandwich
Tell me again how I can't
Take a pretzel bun, PB, blueberries,
And make this work
Look it's done
And delicious

Irony
Is just that
Not a promise to rectify
What I have wrought
I should not hope
For a snowy make out.

Metaphor
I need one
But I'm the employee.

<u>Cosleeping</u>
Head on my belly
Feet on my chest
The circle of life
Is smelly
And sweet

Living Sculpture
These kids
Are only part
Of my collaborative art portfolio.

A Good Host
Yes, the little lampreys
Seem to really enjoy it
In there
My babies sucking me dry

Consuming Fireball
Nine months gone
Perfect larva gone
No laundry vacuum shower food
Nine months perfect larva gone

Same Nightmare
Why would I be pulling
My own veins out
Of my forearms
With C clamps?

Sirens At Night
I am certain that
The old neighbor
Lady is dead
Or her son is going
Back to jail.
Or both.

<u>Free Spirit</u>
Splash some cold water
On your face they say
Like we're not tiny as mice
Too sparse and wild
To reach the tap full stream

<u>Even Assholes</u>
Everyone
Loves
Very
Deeply

<u>Tipsy Writers</u>
We over emphasize
The drink
I only do this
Every other week
But it's so fun
And stupid

Book Code
The smell of glue
And ink
And paper
So many combinations
I'll never figure it out

Artistic Types
We fuck up our lives
We fuck each other
We drink alone
But we occasionally
Paint and write too

McCafe
There are angled
Decorative fry boxes
Hanging askew
Thats whimsical
Its true.

Poet's Kid At Storytime
Can't sit still.
Has to leave early,
Sometimes screaming.
Inspires horror and admiration.

Jogging Stroller
Yep, I think, this is
What it's going to be like
On supply runs
After the zombies come
Before I steal a horse

Winter Warm
Now run
Not to miss the bus
We spent too much joy
Packing and throwing
Snowballs and giggles
Now run
Not to miss the bus

Sinus Infection
My teeth on the ceiling
Where they fell.

A Denim Curse
All jeans
Are mom jeans now.
It's not them.
It's me.

<u>No, Go</u>
Go search
For someone
Who will banter
With you
While you drive

<u>Domestic Relief</u>
A new apartment.
Nobody yelled at me last night.
Not for anything.

<u>Vengeance</u>
The hero stays his sword.
I slice and dice
Ten different ways.

Broke Parent
My babies
My loves
I spent this for you.

Personal Space
Never underestimate
The delight
Of making your own mess.

Grandma Words
Where can I go
To speak like my grandmother
Not just a remembrance
But a throwdown
You silly goose stink otts sourpuss

You As Subject
Hell hath
Fewer words
Than a writer
Clarifying

Drunk History
How can I encapsulate
For new coworkers
That I have both
Studied Proust
And fisted their mom?

It Gets Better
Come on out
Find love
Find sex
Grow older
Queer is over here
Sunscreen at Pride
Porn windows on Castro
Chocolate for breakfast
Anytime you want

Giants Love Story
Posey is gay
For Lincecum
They embrace on the mound
And the freak's hair
Flies free.

Hitachi
Magic wand
Hallelujah
‘Til your hand burns

<u>Car Dental In A Pinch</u>
I just flossed
With an old hot sauce packet
Bcs the Sharpie cap doinger
Didn't work
After my fingernails
And chewing gum
Also didn't work.

Self Pity
I want to take it
Behind the middle school
And get it pregnant.

Selling Stuff on CraigsList
A woman here to pick up the cabinet
I thought she was here for the free breast pump
So that's what I offered
She declined

Dollar Store
Oh, shit.
There goes fifty bucks
In one basket.

Ideal Subject

Upstanding citizen
Seeking
Functional MRI
And registered nurse
To try DMT
And report all results.

Cold Beer On A Hot Day
It warms us up in the winter
But we forget our woes
Regardless of temperature.

Spring
So full of potential
And mud

Trail Jogging
On a night with no moon
Not wise
But the air!
I stumbled a few times
Maybe in dog poop.
Still, I went.

Pooping With Kids

The door is open.
The house is on fire.
Somebody is bleeding.
Just try and focus
On pushing.

Time To Be Old Now

Disco nap?
Fuck it.
I'm going to bed.

Poor Divorce
I used to be one of you
I used to have brunch
Shop at Baby Gap
I used to not pick up
Free food boxes
In my nice Subaru

Testify, Girl
One after the other
I spoke up
I told the truths
They listened to him

Socially Inappropriate Anguish
I genuinely can't see the hints and signs
Asking me nicely to shut the fuck up.
Can you?

Keep Going
When they punch you in
The face
The neck
The stomach
The knee
The other knee
You know what
Just lie down with a beer sometimes

Beth Mattson is a mother, teacher, and writer living in the Driftless area of Wisconsin with all kinds of beasties.

She is extreeeeeeeeeeeemely grateful for friends, family, students, and you glorious readers of all varieties.

You can find Beth at BethMattson.com or her first novel at OpheliaImmune.com

www.ingramcontent.com/pod-product-compliance
Lightning Source LLC
Chambersburg PA
CBHW020954030426
42339CB00005B/100